CW00522515

20 Answers

Divorce and Remarriage

by Jim Blackburn

*All booklets are published thanks to the
generous support of the members of the
Catholic Truth Society*

CATHOLIC TRUTH SOCIETY
PUBLISHERS TO THE HOLY SEE

ISBN 978 1 78469 140 0

Introduction

God instituted marriage at the creation of humanity so that a husband and a wife may bond together in a lifelong covenant and produce a family. Essential to this most fundamental human relationship are the spouses' union with one another and the indissolubility of their bond, as well as their relationship's ordering to both the good of each other and the procreation of children.

Properly understood, Christian marriage emulates the relationship between Christ and his Church. Each relationship is based on a certain indissoluble oneness; spouses are to love each other as Christ loves the Church, helping each other to be holy for the sake of ultimate union with Christ in heaven. Additionally, marriage's procreative aspect images the divine life-giving love that Christ has for the Church.

Unfortunately, corruption has plagued marriage since ancient times. Today more than ever, many factors impede a *true* marriage from coming into existence, and not a few faithful live in *invalid* marriages. These include both first marriages and remarriages after civil divorces. Until an invalid marriage is convalidated, spouses often must deal with difficult realities such as the inability to receive absolution in confession or to participate in Holy Communion.

Fortunately, the Church has procedures in place to assist couples in making their marriages valid, if possible. First marriages are often convalidated through quite simple procedures, but subsequent marriages usually require lengthier processes involving annulments. The annulment process investigates and officially rules on whether a valid marriage exists. Pope Francis recently reformed the process to make it more streamlined and readily accessible to the faithful. Happily, in some cases, an annulment can clear the way for a remarried person to elevate his new relationship to that of a true Christian marriage.

But not every remarriage can or should be recognised as a true marriage. Indeed, many first marriages ending in civil divorce are still actually valid, indissoluble marriages. In such cases, convalidation of subsequent marriages is simply impossible. Other relationships that attempt to mimic marriage - such as same-sex "marriages" - are actually quite offensive to the institution of marriage itself and must always be avoided. Knowing about such issues in advance can help to guard against the error of entering into them in the first place.

To this end, Christians must always approach marriage and the family as an image of Christ and the Church - as the "domestic Church". It is my hope that this booklet will help equip Catholics and other Christians to validly enter into authentic marriages that are divorce-proof for life. By approaching marriage and the family as the image of Christ and the Church, may couples grow to appreciate and embrace the beautiful reality that their relationships truly are.

1. What is marriage?

Catholic teaching on marriage may be best understood by tracing its history through the Bible, as the theme of marriage is quite prevalent throughout Scripture. In fact, the first chapter of Genesis and the final chapter of Revelation bookend Scripture with marriage imagery. The *Catechism* describes the Bible's characterisations of marriage in this way: "Scripture speaks throughout of marriage and its mystery, its institution and the meaning God has given it, its origin and its end, its various realisations throughout the history of salvation, the difficulties arising from sin, and its renewal in the Lord in the New Covenant of Christ and the Church" (1602).

When God created humanity he immediately instituted marriage. This is evidenced in the first two chapters of the Bible: "So God created man in his own image, in the image of God he created him; male and female he created them... Therefore a man leaves his father and his mother and cleaves to his wife, and they become one flesh" (*Gn* 1:27; 2:24). That man is created "male and female" so that husband and wife may bond intimately with each other is abundantly evident here. And seemingly implied in the phrase "they become one flesh" is also the fact that God originally intended marriage to be a lifelong relationship. Husband and wife enter a covenantal relationship that serves to make a new family. From the beginning God intended marriage to be a lifelong commitment, as his displeasure with divorce makes clear: "For I hate divorce, says the Lord the God of Israel" (*Ml* 2:16). Even so, corruptions infiltrated the institution of marriage even in ancient Israel. Such offenses as polygamy and divorce crept in among the chosen people. Due to Israel's difficulty in keeping God's law, the Mosaic Law made concessions for divorce and remarriage (cf. *Dt* 24:1-4). Jesus later lamented these concessions - "I gave them statutes that were not good" (*Ez* 20:25) - and ultimately corrected them:

> Pharisees came up to him and tested him by asking, "Is it lawful to divorce one's wife for any cause?" He answered, "Have you not read that he who made them from the beginning made them male and female, and said, 'For this reason a man shall leave his father and mother and be joined to his wife, and the two shall become one flesh'? So they are no longer two but one flesh. What therefore God has joined together, let not man put asunder." They said to him, "Why then did Moses command one to give a certificate of divorce, and to put her away?" He said to them, "For your hardness of heart Moses allowed you to divorce your wives, but from the beginning it was not so" (*Mt* 19:3-8; cf. *Mk* 10:2-9; *Lk* 16:18).

For his followers, Jesus put things back the way they originally were supposed to be. The *Catechism* explains, "Jesus unequivocally taught the original meaning of the union of man and woman as the Creator willed it from the beginning ...The matrimonial union of man and woman is indissoluble: God himself has determined it" (1614). St Paul recognised this in his teachings as well (cf. *Rm* 7:2-3). The indissolubility of marriage was part of Jesus's fulfilment (i.e., perfection) of the Old Law, of which he said, "Think not that I have come to abolish the law and the prophets; I have come not to abolish them but to fulfil them" (*Mt* 5:17).

But Jesus went even further by enlivening marriage between the baptised with sacramental graces, making it supernaturally life-giving for the spouses themselves. In essence, Christian marriage emulates the relationship between Christ and his Church. This is probably most evident in Paul's letter to the Ephesians, where he writes,

Husbands, love your wives, as Christ loved the Church and gave himself up for her, that he might sanctify her, having cleansed her by the washing of water with the word, that he might present the Church to himself in splendour, without spot or wrinkle or any such thing, that she might be holy and without blemish. Even so husbands should love their wives as their own bodies. He who loves his wife loves himself. For no man ever hates his own flesh, but nourishes and cherishes it, as Christ does the Church, because we are members of his body (5:25-30).

Christ's love for his Church is the ultimate image of what Christian marriage should look like. It is lifelong (indissoluble) and life-giving (procreative and sacramental). Thus, the *Catechism* teaches, "The matrimonial covenant, by which a man and a woman establish between themselves a partnership of the whole of life and which is ordered by its nature to the good of the spouses and the procreation and education of offspring, has been raised by Christ the Lord to the dignity of a sacrament between the baptised" (1601, quoting the *Code of Canon Law* 1055 §1).

2. What specific attributes are inherent to the institution of marriage itself?

Certain *properties* (characteristics or attributes) are inherent to the nature of the marriage relationship. The *Code of Canon Law* states, "The essential properties of marriage are unity and indissolubility, which in Christian marriage obtain a special firmness by reason of the sacrament" (1056). Since marriage should be an image of Christ's relationship with his Church, it is especially revealing to look to *that* relationship to understand these two essential properties.

As we have already seen, tracing marriage through the Bible reveals much about its nature. The same may be said regarding Christ's relationship with the Church. Like marriage itself, God's relationship with his people has a history rooted in the Old Testament. For example, the prophets allegorically remember God's relationship with Israel in nuptial terms: "I will greatly rejoice in the Lord, my soul shall exult in my God; for he has clothed me with the garments of salvation, he has covered me with the robe of righteousness, as a bridegroom decks himself with a garland, and as a bride adorns herself with her jewels" (*Is* 61:10; see also 49:18 and 62:5).

The Israelites' unfaithfulness to God, however, leads to their exile, leaving God yearning like a faithful husband for his beloved wife: "I remember the devotion of your youth, your love as a bride, how you followed me in the wilderness, in a land not sown" (*Jr* 2:2).

Nuptial imagery is especially employed as an allegory for God's relationship with Israel in the book of Hosea. Here *adultery* is explicitly used as a metaphor for Israel's *idolatry*. Hosea's marriage to a "wife of harlotry" (*Ho* 1:2) and an "adulteress" (*Ho* 3:1) is presented, through his actions and his writings, as a prophetic sign to the idolatrous Israelites of their own relationship with God.

Clearly, God's relationship with Israel is depicted in nuptial terms in the Old Testament. And just as the corruption of marriage among the Israelites set the stage for Christ's renewal of marriage, so Israel's unfaithfulness to God set the stage for the development, in Christ, of God's relationship with his people. A more perfect union would be realised in the fullness of God's relationship with all humanity: the marriage of Christ and his Church. This nuptial perfection is inaugurated in the age of the Church and will be fully realised in the kingdom of heaven. The *Catechism* states, "The nuptial covenant between God and his people Israel had prepared the way for the new and everlasting covenant in which the Son of God, by becoming incarnate and giving his life, has united to himself in a certain way all mankind saved by him, thus preparing for the 'wedding-feast of the Lamb'" (1612).

Indeed, at the beginning of his public ministry, Jesus is introduced by John the Baptist with nuptial imagery: "You yourselves bear me witness that I said, I am not the Christ, but I have been sent before him. He who has the bride is the bridegroom" (*Jn* 3:28-29). Jesus also refers to himself in nuptial language in the parable of the wise and the foolish maidens (see *Mt* 25:1-20), and he identifies himself as the bridegroom of his followers (*Mk* 2:18-20). St Paul likewise refers to the church at Corinth in nuptial terms: "I feel a divine jealousy for you, for I betrothed you to Christ to present you as a pure bride to her one husband" (*2 Co* 11:2).

Thus, we see a development in God's relationship with his people much as we see marriage itself develop in the

New Testament. It is no longer a matter of God and the Jews in a volatile union tarnished by the bride's frequent infidelity leading to division and exile. Union between Christ and his Church is an everlasting union focused on the Church being one with Christ. It is this new covenantal relationship which Christian marriage must image. Christ's love for his Church is singular, and the relationship is enduring. Therefore, Christian marriage must be *unifying* as an image of Christ's love, and it must be *indissoluble* as Christ's relationship with his Church is enduring.

Regarding unity, Christian marriage must be based on a certain *oneness* (see *Gn* 2:24; *Mt* 19:5) between the spouses, each loving the other as Christ loves the Church. The *Catechism* makes this point: "Since God created him man and woman, their mutual love becomes an image of the absolute and unfailing love with which God loves man" (1604). In practical terms, this means that the couple must enter into the marriage intending to be faithful to one another.

Concerning indissolubility, Jesus clearly taught that Christian marriage is a lifelong covenant: "What therefore God has joined together, let no man put asunder" (*Mt* 19:6). As the *Catechism* notes, Christ refers in this context to the teaching of Genesis that a man should "cleave" to his wife, and that the two become "one flesh" (*Mt* 2:24): "The Lord himself shows that this signifies an unbreakable union of their two lives by recalling what the plan of the Creator had been in the beginning" (*CCC* 1605). Civil divorce, then, cannot dissolve a Christian marriage. (More on this later.) Therefore, the Catholic Church teaches unequivocally that both the unity and indissolubility of marriage are essential properties of the union itself:

> The love of the spouses requires, of its very nature, the unity and indissolubility of the spouses' community of persons, which embraces their entire life: so they are no longer two, but one flesh. They are called to grow continually in their communion through day-to-day fidelity to their marriage promise of total mutual self-giving (*CCC* 1644).

This being the case, the *Code of Canon Law* recognises the absolute necessity of these properties for a valid marriage to come into existence: "If, however, either or both of the parties by a positive act of the will exclude ...[an] essential property of marriage, the party contracts invalidly" (1101 §2).

3. What purposes of marriage are essential in order for a marriage to be valid?

In addition to the essential properties of unity and indissolubility, marriage also necessarily entails two *elements* (i.e., ends or purposes) that are essential to its validity: its being ordered both to the good of the spouses and to the procreation of offspring.

Looking once again at the history of God's relationship with his people, we see that it finally developed fully in God's sending his Son as Messiah to *redeem* the Jews and expand his kingdom to include all nations in the Church. This Redemption was made by the Bridegroom's self-sacrifice on the cross for his bride so that she may be made perfect, as can be seen in explicit terms in St Paul's letter to the Ephesians: "Christ loved the Church and gave himself up for her, that he might sanctify her, having cleansed her by the washing of water with the word, that he might present the Church to himself in splendour, without spot or wrinkle or any such thing, that she might be holy and without blemish" (5:25-27). Thus, Jesus provides the means for his bride, the Church, to be made perfectly holy.

Later, St John is privileged to view nuptial images of God and the Church in heaven. He relates the joyful words of the multitude gathered there: "'Let us rejoice and exult and give him the glory, for the marriage of the Lamb has come, and his bride has made herself ready; it was granted her to be clothed with fine linen, bright and pure' - for the fine linen is the righteous deeds of the saints" (*Rv* 19:7-8).

Just as Christ makes the Church holy, spouses in human marriage are to help each other to become holy for the sake of ultimate union with Christ in heaven. The *Catechism* teaches, "This human communion is confirmed, purified, and completed by communion in Jesus Christ, given through the sacrament of matrimony. It is deepened by lives of the common faith and by the Eucharist received together" (1644).

In concrete terms, this means that Christian spouses must make each other's salvation a primary end of the relationship itself. Indeed, authentic love between Christian spouses must always be focused on heaven. Christian spouses must see each other as God does: created primarily for union with *him*. Issues of faith and morals must be addressed as the Church addresses them for the sake of each other's salvation.

Since Christian marriage is a sacrament, it is necessarily an instrument of sanctifying grace (i.e., supernatural life). Human marriage is therefore a *salvifi* representation of Christ and his Church. This is of profound significance to married Christians! Members of the Body of Christ are instruments of salvation for their spouses. Spouses resemble Christ in their own marriages.

It's worth keeping in mind that Christian marriage is intended only for this life. Jesus said of human beings after the Resurrection, "They neither marry nor are given in marriage, but are like angels in heaven" (*Mk* 12:25). This makes perfect sense given that the duration of marriage mirrors its salvific purpose - salvific instruments are of use in this life, but they are of no use at all in heaven. Christian marriage not only mirrors Christ's relationship with his Church, but eventually *becomes*, or is transfigured into, that relationship. Thus, Christian marriage takes the shape of a sacrament, in which salvation is inaugurated and partially realised in the present life. In this way it is ordained to the good of the spouses.

Additionally, in being ordered to procreation, Christian marriage is an image of the divine live-giving marriage of Christ and the Church. The *Catechism* teaches, "In the procreation and education of children [the family] reflects the Father's work of creation" (2205). And just as Christ is always creating new life in the Church (i.e., through baptism; see Jn 3:1-7), so also human marriage is ordered to creating new life. Marriage must be life-giving in this regard as an image of Christ's marriage to his Church, through which he makes each Christian a new creation (see *2 Co* 5:17) and a partaker of his own divine life (see *2 Pt* 1:4).

Because of this life-giving aspect of Christian marriage, every couple must necessarily consist of one male and one female (see also answer 18), as that is how God created human beings to multiply; indeed, the primary reason God created human beings male and female is for the purpose of procreation. For a couple to put up an obstacle to this essential element of marriage is for them to turn their backs on their marriage's nature as an image of Christ and his Church. The Catholic Church teaches unequivocally on this matter. The *Catechism* teaches, "Every action which, whether in anticipation of the conjugal act, or in its accomplishment, or in the development of its natural consequences, proposes, whether as an end or as a means, to render procreation impossible is intrinsically evil" (2370, quoting from *Humanae Vitae*). Contraception in marriage is therefore immoral.

Once again, the Church's *Code of Canon Law* emphasises these life-giving elements of marriage, stating that marriage "is ordered by its nature to the good of the spouses and the procreation and education of offspring" (1055 §1) and affirming their necessity in order for a valid marriage to come into existence: "If, however, either or both of the parties by a positive act of the will exclude ...some essential element of marriage...the party contracts invalidly" (1101 §2).

4. How does the Catholic Church view mixed marriages and marriages to non-Christians?

Until now, our attention has been primarily focused on marriage between two Catholics. But what does the Church say about marriage between a Catholic and a non-Catholic Christian? And what about marriage between a Catholic and a non-Christian? What does the Church say about these two types of marriages in comparison with Catholic marriage?

Since marriages between Catholics, united in the same faith, are those which most closely image Christ's relationship with the Church, certainly they are to be preferred to any others. In fact, the closer two spouses come to sharing the fullness of the Christian faith (i.e., the Catholic faith), the better they can each mirror Christ to one another in their marriage. Indeed, the Catholic Church maintains a strong preference that Catholics marry other Catholics. When a Catholic marries a non-Catholic Christian - forming what is known as a "mixed marriage" - the spouses do not *fully* share the same beliefs, nor are they equipped to fully pass along *one* confession of faith to their children. When a Catholic marries a non-Christian - forming what is known as a "disparity of cult marriage" - the difficulties are further compounded. Consequently, the *Catechism* points out that a mixed marriage "requires particular attention on the part of couples and their pastors," and that a disparity of cult marriage "requires even greater circumspection" (1633). The *Catechism* goes on to explain some of the reasons for this:

> The difficulties of mixed marriages must not be underestimated. They arise from the fact that the separation of Christians has not yet been overcome. The spouses risk experiencing the tragedy of Christian disunity even in the heart of their own home. Disparity of cult can further aggravate these difficulties. Differences about faith and the very notion of marriage, but also different religious mentalities, can become sources of tension in marriage, especially as regards the education of children. The temptation to religious indifference can then arise (1634).

Because of these difficulties, the Catholic Church has put in place laws to ensure that due consideration is given whenever a Catholic wishes to marry a non-Catholic. In addition to observation of the appropriate form of marriage (see answer 5 below), the *Code of Canon Law* requires the Catholic party to obtain either express permission or an express dispensation from his bishop to enter into such a marriage (1124). If he wishes to enter into a mixed marriage, express permission is necessary for liceity (i.e., legality) but not necessarily validity. On the other hand, if he wishes to enter into a disparity of cult marriage, an express dispensation is necessary for both the liceity *and the validity* of the marriage. This is important to keep in mind since an invalid marriage is not truly a marriage at all.

The *Code* goes on to explain the conditions necessary for such permission or such a dispensation to be granted:

The local ordinary can grant a permission [or a dispensation] of this kind if there is a just and reasonable cause. He is not to grant it unless the following conditions have been fulfilled:

1. the Catholic party is to declare that he or she is prepared to remove dangers of defecting from the faith and is to make a sincere promise to do all in his or her power so that all offspring are baptised and brought up in the Catholic Church;

2. the other party is to be informed at an appropriate time about the promises which the Catholic party is to make, in such a way that it is certain that he or she is truly aware of the promise and obligation of the Catholic party;

3. both parties are to be instructed about the purposes and essential properties of marriage which neither of the contracting parties is to exclude (*CIC* 1125).

None of this is to imply that mixed marriages and disparity of cult marriages cannot be good marriages. Indeed, they can be. But it is important that both spouses understand what they are getting into and, especially in regard to Catholic parties, that they are prepared to fulfil their obligations as spouses and parents. To this end, regarding mixed marriages, the *Catechism* exhorts bishops and other pastors to ensure the necessary spiritual help (1128) and later states, "Difference of confession between the spouses does not constitute an insurmountable obstacle for marriage, when they succeed in placing in common what they have received from their respective communities, and learn from each other the way in which each lives in fidelity to Christ" (1634).

Finally, concerning disparity of cult marriages, the *Catechism* reminds the Catholic spouse that he has a particular task concerning his non-Christian spouse:

"For the unbelieving husband is consecrated through his wife, and the unbelieving wife is consecrated through her husband" (*1 Co* 7:16). It is a great joy for the Christian spouse and for the Church if this "consecration" should lead to the free conversion of the other spouse to the Christian faith. Sincere married love, the humble and patient practice of the family virtues, and perseverance in prayer can prepare the non-believing spouse to accept the grace of conversion (*CCC* 1637).

5. What is the Catholic "form" of marriage, and why is it important?

The Catholic "form" of marriage (canonical form) refers to certain aspects of the wedding itself. When a Catholic gets married, he ordinarily must observe certain requirements in order for his marriage to be valid. These usually entail, among other things, that a marriage be contracted before certain witnesses. The *Code of Canon Law* explains, "Only those marriages are valid which are contracted before the local ordinary, pastor, or a priest or deacon delegated by either of them, who assist, and before two witnesses" (1108 §1).

Additionally, the law states, "The form...must be observed if at least one of the parties contracting the marriage was baptised in the Catholic Church or received into it" (1117). This law is imposed by the authority endowed upon the Church by Jesus (see below). Thus, a Catholic ordinarily *must* observe canonical form in order for his marriage to be valid.

If a Catholic wishes to validly marry any other way he must first obtain from his bishop a dispensation from the Catholic canonical form. (This is ordinarily handled through his local pastor.) If he fails to obtain a dispensation and proceeds with a wedding apart from the Church, his wedding lacks canonical form and his marriage is not valid. An exception to this general rule exists in the case of a Catholic who marries a non-Catholic Christian of an Eastern rite, such as an Eastern Orthodox Christian, observing that rite's form of marriage. In such a case, failure to obtain a dispensation is illicit but does not invalidate the marriage.

Why does the Church impose a law that Catholics normally are to be married according to the canonical form? The *Catechism* explains,

Several reasons converge to explain this requirement:

- Sacramental marriage is a liturgical act. It is therefore appropriate that it should be celebrated in the public liturgy of the Church;

- Marriage introduces one into an ecclesial order and creates rights and duties in the Church between the spouses and towards their children;

- Since marriage is a state of life in the Church, certainty about it is necessary (hence the obligation to have witnesses);

- The public character of the consent protects the "I do" once given and helps the spouses remain faithful to it (1631).

Sometimes questions arise about the grave necessity of observing the canonical form of marriage. How can the Church impose a law that *must* be observed for a marriage to be valid? It is important to remember that Jesus gave the Church the authority to enact laws that bind the faithful. He said to St Peter (the first pope) and then later to all of the apostles, "Whatever you bind on earth shall be bound in heaven and whatever you loose on earth shall be loosed in heaven" (*Mt* 16:19; 18:18). The *Catechism* comments,

> The power to "bind and loose" connotes the authority to absolve sins, to pronounce doctrinal judgements, and to make disciplinary decisions in the Church. Jesus entrusted this authority to the Church through the ministry of the apostles and in particular through the ministry of Peter, the only one to whom he specifically entrusted the keys of the kingdom (553; emphasis added).

This being the case, the Church authoritatively states in the *Code of Canon Law*, "Merely ecclesiastical laws [i.e., those that are Church-imposed, as in CIC 1117] bind those who have been baptised in the Catholic Church or received into it, possess the efficient use of reason, and, unless the law expressly provides otherwise, have completed seven years of age" (11).

In addition to the explicit form required above, the Church also recognises the appropriateness of certain other aspects of the wedding. For example, it is most fitting that a wedding between two Catholics take place within the context of the Mass. It is in the Mass, after all, that we remember the nuptial relationship between Christ and the Church, which the marriage being celebrated should mirror. The *Catechism* explains,

> In the Eucharist the memorial of the New Covenant is realised, the New Covenant in which Christ has united himself for ever to the Church, his beloved bride for whom he gave himself up. It is therefore fitting that the spouses should seal their consent to give themselves to each other through the offering of their own lives by uniting it to the offering of Christ for his Church made present in the Eucharistic sacrifice, and by receiving the Eucharist so that, communicating in the same body and the same blood of Christ, they may form but "one body" in Christ (1621).

Finally, it is appropriate that the bride and groom go to confession before the wedding so that they may be properly disposed for the Sacrament of Matrimony (see *CCC* 1622), which they mutually confer upon each other (see *CCC* 1623).

6. What other factors may invalidate a marriage?

We have already addressed several factors that prevent a valid marriage from coming into existence: exclusion of an essential property of marriage (answer 2), exclusion of an essential element of marriage (answer 3), failure to obtain a dispensation to enter into a disparity of cult marriage (answer 4), and defect of form (answer 5).

In addition to these, the *Code of Canon Law* lists several other "diriment impediments", any one of which "renders a person unqualified to contract marriage validly" (1073). Some of these arise from a person's incapacity to enter into marriage, others from a person's legal disqualification to marry. Some are permanent, others temporary. Some are a matter of divine law and, therefore, cannot be dispensed (i.e., officially "waived"). Others are a matter of ecclesiastical (Church-imposed) law and may sometimes be dispensed by proper authorities.

Some impediments are obvious. For example, those who are incapable of consenting to marriage - including persons who lack sufficient use of reason or judgement, or who suffer from a psychological illness impairing their free will - are incapable of marriage itself.

If a person is already married, he is incapable of marrying someone else. Similarly, a person in holy orders (deacon, priest, or bishop) is incapable of marriage. This is true even in cases in which the person was ordained as a married man but has become a widower. Additionally, a person who is bound by a vow of celibacy (e.g., a nun or a religious priest) is incapable of marriage.

The Church also rules out the validity of certain marriages involving the kidnapping of someone in order to forcefully bring about a marriage, or the murder of a spouse in order to free one person to marry another. Similarly, certain types of deception prevent a valid marriage from coming into existence. Fear, too, can constitute an impediment, as canon law states, "A marriage is invalid if entered into because of force or grave fear from without, even if unintentionally inflicted, so that a person is compelled to choose marriage in order to be free from it" (*CIC* 1103).

Marriages between family members too closely related are invalid. For example, first cousins cannot validly marry each other (although this impediment may be dispensed). No one is capable of marrying a person who is related in the "direct line" (e.g., a grandparent, parent, child, or grandchild; this impediment may never be dispensed).

Other impediments are not immediately quite so obvious. For example, the Church has universally established a minimum legal age of sixteen for a man and fourteen for a woman to validly marry. Since girls ordinarily begin maturing at an earlier age than boys do, it makes sense that the minimum age for each should be different. Note that the ages established are the *minimum* allowed anywhere in the world, although each conference of bishops may choose to establish a higher minimum age within their own territory.

The *Code of Canon Law states*, "A marriage subject to a condition about the future cannot be contracted validly" (1102 §1). This excludes the possibility of a valid marriage subject to a prenuptial agreement.

Finally, a person who is incapable of engaging in sexual intercourse (e.g., is impotent) is incapable of marriage. This impediment applies equally to men and to women. It makes sense given that one of the essential elements of marriage is its ordination to the procreation of offspring. If a person is physically incapable of even consummating a marriage, he is incapable of marriage itself. It is important, though, to distinguish between impotence and sterility. Sterility does not necessarily render a person incapable of intercourse and therefore does not, of itself, invalidate a marriage.

In view of all of these factors that prevent a valid marriage from coming into existence, a word of caution is in order: the Church presumes the validity of marriage unless some invalidating factor is explicitly proven in the Church's external forum (through the annulment process). The *Code of Canon Law* states, "Marriage possesses the favour of law; therefore, in a case of doubt, the validity of a marriage must be upheld until the contrary is proven" (1060). Therefore, spouses should be cautious not to fall into a sort of hypochondria concerning the validity of their marriage. Rather, they ordinarily should rest in the presumption - as the Church does - that their marriage is valid. Only when there is some clearly invalidating factor, such as defect of form, should a couple become concerned.

7. Is there a way for an invalid marriage to be made valid?

It is not uncommon today for a fallen-away Catholic who married outside the Church, neither observing the required form of marriage nor obtaining a dispensation from that form, to desire to return to the Church. This might happen, for instance, when his first child is born and he desires to have his child baptised and raised in the Church. Upon looking into the matter, he finds out that his marriage is not valid due to a defect of form, and he is unable not only to have his child baptised but even to receive any sacraments himself as long as he remains actively living as though he were in a valid marriage. What is he to do?

Fortunately, the Church has the necessary procedures in place to help Catholics in invalid marriages to get their marriages validated (if possible). These two procedures are known as a simple convalidation and radical sanation.

When a marriage is invalid due to defect of form, the couple must exchange their wedding vows again, this time observing the Catholic form of marriage, in order for their marriage to be made valid. The *Code of Canon Law* states,

"A marriage which is null because of defect of form must be contracted anew in canonical form in order to become valid" (1160). In practical terms, this simply means that the couple must appear before an official witness of the Church - usually a deacon or priest - along with two other witnesses of their choice, and renew their wedding vows.

Of course, there are other reasons a marriage may be invalid, so the Church has procedures to assist in those situations as well. In the case of a marriage that is null due to a diriment impediment, before the marriage may be convalidated it is first necessary to make certain that the impediment no longer exists or has been officially dispensed. In such a case, canon law requires that "at least the party conscious of the impediment renews consent" (1156 §1). If both spouses are aware of the impediment, "both parties must renew the consent in canonical form" (1158 §1). Either way, the spouse(s) aware of the impediment must *newly* consent to the marriage - consent, that is, with a "new act of the will" (*CIC* 1157) - even if original lack of consent is not the impediment itself.

When a convalidation is performed as described above, technically, the couple's marriage comes into existence at the time of the renewal of consent by either or both spouses. They are newly married at the time of the convalidation. Indeed, some couples choose to celebrate their wedding anniversaries on *that* date from then on because, in the eyes of God and the Church, that is when they truly got married.

This can be a new cause of great joy for the couple.

On the other hand, it sometimes happens - especially in cases of mixed marriages and disparity of cult marriages - that one of the spouses does not recognise the Church's authority concerning marriage and might not wish to participate in the convalidation process at all. The Catholic spouse might ask, "Can my marriage be convalidated without the co-operation of my spouse?" Radical sanation is often the answer.

Radical sanation is the *retroactive* validation of an invalid marriage. In fact, the Latin roots of "radical sanation" literally mean "healing in the root". Such a convalidation does not require renewal of consent provided the consent of both spouses has been there all along and the marriage is on good terms. If the consent of either spouse was ever lacking, the convalidation is retroactive only as far back as both spouses have consented to the marriage. Of course, as with simple convalidation, diriment impediments must be removed or dispensed before radical sanation can happen. The *Code of Canon Law* states,

§1. The radical sanation of an invalid marriage is its convalidation without the renewal of consent, which is granted by competent authority and entails the dispensation from an impediment, if there is one, and from canonical form, if it was not observed, and the retroactivity of canonical effects.

§2. Convalidation occurs at the moment of the granting of the favour. Retroactivity, however, is understood to extend to the moment of the celebration of the marriage unless other provision is expressly made.

§3. A radical sanation is not to be granted unless it is probable that the parties wish to persevere in conjugal life (1161).

It is worth noting here that the Church can dispense from impediments imposed only by ecclesiastical law, not divine law. This being the case, a marriage that is invalid due to a diriment impediment imposed by divine law cannot be convalidated unless that impediment first ceases to exist.

8. What does the Church teach about divorce?

We saw above (see answer 1) that corruption of God's plan for marriage entered into the world even among the ancient Israelites and that Jesus restored marriage among his followers to the way it was originally intended. Unfortunately, in many cultures today, God's plan for marriage has been corrupted again as the governing of marriage has been handed over to civil authorities, most of whom assume they have the power to dissolve marriages. Civil divorce is often thought to free spouses of their nuptial bonds so that they may go on to marry others.

Consistent with Jesus's teaching (see *Mt* 19:3-9), the Catholic Church continues to teach both the indissolubility of marriage and the gravity of divorce. The *Catechism* teaches,

> *Divorce* is a grave offense against the natural law. It claims to break the contract, to which the spouses freely consented, to live with each other till death. Divorce does injury to the covenant of salvation, of which sacramental marriage is the sign. Contracting a new union, even if it is recognised by civil law, adds to the gravity of the rupture: the remarried spouse is then in a situation of public and permanent adultery: If a husband, separated from his wife, approaches another woman, he is an adulterer because he makes that woman commit adultery, and the woman who lives with him is an adulteress, because she has drawn another's husband to herself (2384).

Note that the *Catechism* does not say divorce dissolves marriage but that it "claims to break the contract". Civil authorities simply do not have the power to dissolve a Christian marriage. And since Christian marriage is to be a human image of Christ's relationship with his Church, civil divorce seriously corrupts that image. When a divorced spouse goes on to civilly marry another, he enters into an adulterous relationship with someone who is not truly his spouse. This is a grave situation for both of them, but as the

Catechism points out, it also harms the people around them: "Divorce is immoral also because it introduces disorder into the family and into society. This disorder brings grave harm to the deserted spouse, to children traumatised by the separation of their parents and often torn between them, and because of its contagious effect which makes it truly a plague on society" (2385).

Even so, in many societies today, so-called no-fault divorce means that one spouse may civilly divorce the other through no fault of the latter's. Does this type of divorce constitute a sin on the part of the spouse who does not choose it? Of course, the answer is no. The Church addresses this question in the *Catechism*:

> It can happen that one of the spouses is the innocent victim of a divorce decreed by civil law; this spouse therefore has not contravened the moral law. There is a considerable difference between a spouse who has sincerely tried to be faithful to the sacrament of marriage and is unjustly abandoned, and one who through his own grave fault destroys a canonically valid marriage (2386).

But what about a spouse who *does* choose civil divorce as a way to protect himself, his children, or his assets, from an unjust spouse? If divorce is chosen as a necessary protection but is not viewed as a dissolution of the marriage, then it may be a legitimate form of legal separation.

The *Catechism* states, "The separation of spouses while maintaining the marriage bond can be legitimate in certain cases provided for by canon law. If civil divorce remains the only possible way of ensuring certain legal rights, the care of the children, or the protection of inheritance, it can be tolerated and does not constitute a moral offense" (2383).

However, it is important to make clear that civil divorce does nothing in regard to the validity of a marriage. Even though civil authorities may claim that a marriage has been broken and the spouses are free to marry others, this is simply not the truth of the matter. The only legitimate authority governing Christian marriages is Christ, through his Church. This is not to say that Christians should not co-operate with civil authorities insofar as their actions are legitimate (e.g., issuing marriage licenses under the competence of the state), but Christians must never concede to civil authorities that authority which belongs to God and the Church alone. As Jesus proclaimed, "What therefore God has joined together, let no man put asunder" (*Mt* 19:6).

9. What about the so-called "exception clause" for divorce in the case of adultery?

Some non-Catholic Christians hold that Jesus made an exception to the rule of marriage's indissolubility when he said that "whoever divorces his wife, *except for unchastity*, and marries another commits adultery"

(*Mt* 19:9, emphasis added; see also *Mt* 5:31-32). Many even translate the phrase "except for unchastity" as "except for adultery." This notion then opens the door to divorce and remarriage whenever one spouse cheats on the other. If one spouse is unfaithful, the couple may proceed to divorce and remarriage. One could even argue that if one spouse wanted to divorce for *any* reason, he could simply commit adultery, thereby breaking the bond of indissolubility and freeing himself to divorce and marry another.

This logic is quite problematic for a number of reasons. First, both Jesus's and St Paul's constant, forceful teaching about the permanence of sacramental marriage as recorded elsewhere in Scripture makes clear that Jesus was not making an exception to indissolubility in the case of valid, consummated marriages. Nowhere else in the New Testament do we find any sort of "exception" to the rule of indissolubility.

Additionally, the Church Fathers were quite adamant that, even if unchastity in the case of a valid marriage led to divorce, it did not break the bond of indissolubility or free the spouses to remarry others. So there must be something else going on here.

The most likely solution hinges on precisely what is meant by "unchastity". Certainly adultery falls under the umbrella of unchastity, but it seems that Jesus had something else in mind. The Greek word translated as "unchastity" is *porneia* (from which the word *pornography* is derived), and its literal meaning is certainly broader than just marital unfaithfulness. Indeed, if Jesus had intended to single out adultery, Matthew could simply have used the word *moicheia* here, which was the ordinary Greek word for adultery. But that's not what the text says.

Another place where the word *porneia* is found in the New Testament is in the first letter of St Paul to the Corinthians: "It is actually reported that there is immorality among you, and of a kind that is not found even among pagans; for a man is living with his father's wife" (*1 Co* 5:1). In this verse, *porneia* is translated as "immorality", but Paul clearly explains what he means by it: "a man is living with his father's wife." In other words, a form of *incest* is being practised. Jewish law prohibited such behaviour, (see *Lv* 18:8) and, of course, Christianity does, too.

If Jesus intended to convey a meaning similar to Paul's, then his words "except for unchastity" referred to sexual immorality *between the husband and wife themselves*. It might be helpful to recognise that Matthew's Gospel was written to an audience predominately consisting of Christian converts from Judaism. As we have seen, first-century Judaism did not understand marriage in quite the way God had intended it from the beginning. Marriage laws were less than ideal and sometimes even ignored. Even laws in the book of Leviticus prohibiting marriage between close relatives (see *Lv* 18:6-18) were not always followed.

It seems likely, then, that Jesus was teaching Jewish disciples who thought that, in cases in which a couple should not have married each other in the first place, divorce and remarriage would be allowed. Strictly speaking, couples who are too closely related to have validly married in the first place are not truly in a marriage anyway, and therefore they actually *should* end their sexual relationship and be free to marry other spouses. This course of action is actually not unlike an annulment (more on annulments later).

10. What does the Church teach about *remarriage* after divorce?

It is important to recognise that in Jesus's teaching about marriage and divorce, he is concerned with the erroneous presumption that divorce - for any reason - actually *ends* a marriage in such a way that it frees the spouses to go on to marry others. He said to his disciples, "Whoever divorces his wife and marries another commits adultery against her; and if she divorces her husband and marries another, she commits adultery" (*Mk* 10:11-12).

St Paul's teaching agrees with Jesus's: "To the married I give charge, not I but the Lord, that the wife should not separate from her husband (but if she does, let her remain single or else be reconciled to her husband) - and that the husband should not divorce his wife" (*1 Co* 7:10-11).

Paul understood that divorce is a terrible thing, yet it is sometimes a reality (see answer 8). But in any case, divorce does not end an indissoluble marriage, nor does it free the spouses to marry others.

Thus, the *Catechism* teaches,

> Today there are numerous Catholics in many countries who have recourse to civil *divorce* and contract new civil unions. In fidelity to the words of Jesus Christ - "Whoever divorces his wife and marries another, commits adultery against her; and if she divorces her husband and marries another, she commits adultery" - the Church maintains that a new union cannot be recognised as valid, if the first marriage was. If the divorced are remarried civilly, they find themselves in a situation that objectively contravenes God's law (1650).

Their situation contravenes God's law because they are still married to their first spouses. To live as though they are married to others is to live in a state of adultery because civil divorce does not - indeed, cannot - truly end an indissoluble marriage. The *Catechism* goes on to clarify, "The remarriage of persons divorced from a living, lawful spouse contravenes the plan and law of God as taught by Christ" (1665).

Note the mention of "a living" spouse. It is important to remember that although divorce does not end an indissoluble marriage, death does (see answer 8). Paul makes this point in the book of Romans:

> Do you not know, brethren - for I am speaking to those who know the law - that the law is binding on a person only during his life? Thus a married woman is bound by law to her husband as long as he lives; but if her husband dies she is discharged from the law concerning the husband. Accordingly, she will be called an adulteress if she lives with another man while her husband is alive. But if her husband dies she is free from that law, and if she marries another man she is not an adulteress (7:1-3).

Thus, once a spouse dies, the surviving spouse is free to marry someone else.

In light of this teaching on the indissolubility of marriage until death, it makes sense that a Catholic who is divorced from his still-living spouse cannot approach his local pastor to plan a Catholic wedding with another person. Indeed, he cannot do so simply because of the impediment of prior marriage (see answer 6).

Tragically, not a few Catholics who are (or were) unaware of the Church's teaching on divorce have unknowingly contravened God's law in this regard. They have divorced their spouses, gone on to civilly marry other spouses, and even started new families. As in the situation described in answer 7 above, it is often at this stage of beginning to raise a family - and desiring to do so in the

Catholic faith - that they come to discover the mess they have gotten themselves into. All too often, they become overwhelmed by their situations, feeling powerless to correct the mistakes they have made. Although the Church is intent on helping them to live holy lives (more on this below), it also recognises the difficulty of their situations and exhorts the faithful to care for them:

> Toward Christians who live in this situation, and who often keep the faith and desire to bring up their children in a Christian manner, priests and the whole community must manifest an attentive solicitude, so that they do not consider themselves separated from the Church, in whose life they can and must participate as baptised persons:
>
> They should be encouraged to listen to the word of God, to attend the sacrifice of the Mass, to persevere in prayer, to contribute to works of charity and to community efforts for justice, to bring up their children in the Christian faith, to cultivate the spirit and practice of penance and thus implore, day by day, God's grace (*CCC* 1651).

11. May a divorced Catholic receive Communion?

This is a question that has demanded much attention recently, with synods of bishops in Rome taking up precisely this topic (more on this below). Of primary concern here is the situation of a Catholic who is divorced and civilly remarried. Divorce itself, under certain circumstances and apart from subsequent civil remarriage, is not necessarily a sin (see answer 8). Therefore, being divorced is not a barrier to receiving the sacraments, including the Eucharist. Difficulties arise, however, when a divorced Catholic civilly remarries and goes on to live perpetually in an objective state of sin (adultery; see answer 10).

The Church teaches that a Catholic must be in the state of grace (free from the guilt of grave sin) in order to receive the Eucharist. If a baptised person has committed a mortal sin, he ordinarily must make a good confession within the Sacrament of Reconciliation before receiving the Eucharist (see *CCC* 1385). Otherwise he commits the additional grave sin of sacrilege. St Paul warns: "Whoever, therefore, eats the bread or drinks the cup of the Lord in an unworthy manner will be guilty of profaning the body and blood of the Lord. Let a man examine himself, and so eat of the bread and drink of the cup. For anyone who eats and drinks without discerning the body eats and drinks judgement upon himself" (*1 Co* 11:27-29).

In order to receive the Sacrament of Reconciliation, a person must be *contrite*. This means that, in addition to being sorry for his sins, he must have the intention of ceasing his sinful behaviour (see *CCC* 1451). Both of these requirements must ordinarily be met before a person who has committed *any* grave sin may receive the Eucharist: he must repent of - and intend to cease - his sinful behaviour, and he must be forgiven of his sin through the Sacrament of Reconciliation.

These requirements present an obstacle for a person who is divorced and civilly remarried, because he is living in the objective state of adultery, and adultery is both a grave sin (see *CCC* 2400 and 1858) and a perpetual one. The *Catechism* teaches:

> Contracting a new union, even if it is recognised by civil law, adds to the gravity of the rupture [of divorce]: the remarried spouse is then in a situation of public and permanent adultery:
>
> If a husband, separated from his wife, approaches another woman, he is an adulterer because he makes that woman commit adultery, and the woman who lives with him is an adulteress, because she has drawn another's husband to herself (2384).

To receive the Sacrament of Reconciliation, a divorced person who is living in a subsequent invalid marriage ordinarily must repent and intend to cease living as though he is married to his new partner. The *Catechism* teaches, "Reconciliation through the sacrament of penance can be granted only to those who have repented for having violated the sign of the covenant and of fidelity to Christ, and who are committed to living in complete continence" (1650). This means either choosing to live chastely with a current partner or separating altogether, until the situation has been rectified, if possible (see answers 7 and 13). If a person does not intend to live in complete continence, then his grave sins are not forgiven and he is therefore not properly disposed to receive Communion. Indeed, the *Catechism* states that such a person "cannot receive Eucharistic Communion as long as this situation persists" (1650).

During the extraordinary synod of 2014 and the ordinary synod of 2015, the bishops explored the possibility of allowing some divorced and remarried Catholics to be granted absolution through the Sacrament of Reconciliation and then to receive the Eucharist *without* having yet rectified the situations of perpetual adultery. In his post-synodal apostolic exhortation *Amoris Laetitia* (*AL*), Pope Francis points out, "Priests have the duty to accompany the divorced and remarried in helping them to understand their situation according to the teaching of the Church and the guidelines of the bishop" (*AL* 300). He goes on to promote a pastoral approach to such cases, "one which would recognise that, since the degree of responsibility is not equal in all cases, the consequences or effects of a rule need not necessarily always be the same" (*AL* 300).

In other words, in cases of objective grave sin in which subjective culpability is lacking (see *CCC* 1735, 2352) - and therefore mortal sin is not present - the consequences may be different. Pope Francis mentions sacramental discipline in this regard in two footnotes (*AL* footnotes 336, 351), but he does not ever directly state that reception of the Eucharist should be permitted. In fact, he seems to caution against such an understanding. He describes this pastoral approach further, stating: "What we are speaking of is a process of accompaniment and discernment which guides the faithful to an awareness of their situation before God. Conversation with the priest, in the internal forum, contributes to the formation of a correct judgement on what hinders the possibility of a fuller participation in the life of the Church and on what steps can foster it and make it grow ...[T]his discernment can never prescind from the gospel demands of truth and charity, as proposed by the Church" (*AL* 300).

Pope Francis warns that such a pastoral approach must be carried out with caution. "In order to avoid all misunderstanding, I would point out that in no way must the Church desist from proposing the full ideal of marriage, God's plan in all its grandeur... A lukewarm attitude, any kind of relativism, or an undue reticence in proposing that ideal, would be a lack of fidelity to the gospel and also of love on the part of the Church for young people themselves" (*AL* 307).

12. Can any marriages *ever* be dissolved?

A valid, consummated Christian marriage is indissoluble by any power other than death. But what about a marriage that does not quite fit this mould? After all, marriage between two Christians is not the only type of marriage there is (see answer 4). The question naturally arises whether *any* marriage can ever be dissolved for *any* reason at all.

We have already discussed the indissolubility of marriages between Catholics in covenantal relationships imaging Christ's own relationship with his Church. Such indissolubility also applies to mixed marriages as well as marriages between two non-Catholic Christians, since these, too, are marriages between two baptised people and, as such, are sacramental unions. Indeed, the *Code of Canon Law* confirms the indissolubility of marriage among all baptised Christians: "A [Christian] marriage that is [valid and consummated] can be dissolved by no human power and by no cause, except death" (1141).

Notice that consummation is a determining factor in whether or not a Christian marriage is dissoluble. The fact is that any *non-consummated* marriage involving at least one Christian *may* be dissoluble by the pope. The *Code of Canon Law* states, "For a just cause, the Roman pontiff can dissolve a non-consummated marriage between baptised persons or between a baptised party and a non-baptised party at the request of both parties or of one of them, even if the other party is unwilling" (1142). This is sometimes referred to as the "Petrine privilege", named for the first pope, St Peter. Once consummated, though, every valid Christian marriage is indissoluble even by the pope.

But what about a consummated marriage between a Christian and a non-Christian or between two non-Christians (known as a "natural" marriage)? St Paul taught that dissolution of a natural marriage is not desirable (*1 Co* 7:12-14), but he went on to teach that natural marriages may be dissolved in certain circumstances, such as when one of the parties becomes a Christian: "If the unbelieving partner desires to separate, let it be so; in such a case the brother or sister is not bound. For God has called us to peace" (*1 Co* 7:15).

Accordingly, the *Code of Canon Law* provides for the dissolution of natural marriages in those same circumstances as well: "A marriage entered into by two non-baptised persons is dissolved by means of the Pauline privilege [named for St Paul] in favour of the faith of the party who has received baptism by the very fact that a new marriage is contracted by the same party, provided that the non-baptised party departs" (1143 §1).

At first, it might seem as though the Church does not revere natural marriages at all. However, this is not the case. The *Code of Canon Law* goes on to point out the limitations on such dissolutions: "The non-baptised party is considered to depart if he or she does not wish to cohabit with the baptised party or to cohabit peacefully without affront to the Creator unless the baptised party, after baptism was received, has given the other a just cause for departing" (1143 §2). In other words, through no fault of the Christian spouse after his baptism, the non-Christian must either freely leave the marriage or must make living the Christian life difficult for the baptised spouse.

Furthermore, the law requires consultation with the non-Christian spouse before the Christian may go on to marry someone else (*CIC* 1144-1145). The non-Christian spouse ordinarily must be questioned about whether he wishes also to become a Christian or, in any case, to remain married peacefully. He must be given a reasonable period of time to respond. Upon dissolution, the Christian may go on to marry another Catholic or, with the permission of his bishop, a non-Catholic.

Finally, the Church's law even makes provisions for situations in which multiple spouses are concerned, such as in polygamous third-world cultures that have been evangelised by Christians. What is a person with multiple spouses to do when he becomes a Christian? Church law provides for the determination of one legitimate spouse while also ensuring the well-being of the illegitimate ones (see *CIC* 1148 §1-3).

Keep in mind that it was Christ who restored marriage to the meaning God originally intended it to have, and it was he who elevated it to the status of a sacrament among his followers. Inasmuch as all people are called to be Christians, marriages must image the relationship of Christ and his Church. Until all marriages do that, the Church must continue to recognise the reality of lesser relationships in a world still suffering from the consequences of sin and the hardness of hearts. Canon law therefore necessarily and happily includes provisions for dissolving such relationships in favour of entering into new relationships built on the image of Christ and his Church.

13. What is an annulment?

One of the most valuable ways in which the Church assists people in dealing with the difficult reality of divorce is the annulment process. Annulments are sometimes mistakenly referred to as "Catholic divorces". In reality, annulments do not presume to end valid marriages at all, but rather simply recognise and declare, after sufficient investigation, that a valid marriage never existed in the first place. Of course, if a valid marriage never truly existed, then there is nothing to dissolve.

Recognition of this reality then opens the door for a civilly divorced person to go on and marry someone else. His relationship with his first partner has been proven not to have been a marriage, so a future marriage is not impeded by the prior relationship. Additionally, an annulment can empower a divorced and civilly remarried person to rectify his difficult situation (see answers 10 and 11) by opening up the possibility of having his new marriage convalidated (see answer 7). An annulment is a formal declaration that what appears to be a marriage is not one. Such a declaration may be warranted for a number of reasons.

When a couple exchanges consent (at the wedding), either a valid marriage comes into existence at that moment or - if something necessary for a valid marriage is lacking - it does not. Some of the necessary conditions for a valid marriage are due to natural law; others are imposed by the Church's authority. Either way, if even one thing is lacking, the marriage will be null.

In the Catholic Church, canon law generally recognises three ways in which a wedding may fail to bring about a valid marriage: lack of capacity, lack of consent, and lack of form. We have already touched on these in discussing diriment impediments (answer 6), lack of consent to an essential property of marriage (answer 2), lack of consent to an essential element of marriage (answer 3), and lack of form (answer 5). We also pointed out that failure to observe certain ecclesiastical laws - such as the requirement of a dispensation to enter into a disparity of cult marriage (answer 4) - prevents a valid marriage from coming into existence. We will briefly summarise here the three possible reasons for an annulment and then expound on them in answer 14.

In order to validly marry, a person must first be capable of marriage. If he is lacking anything that is required to be capable of marriage, then a wedding will not result in a valid marriage, and thus there will be grounds for annulment. (Revisit answer 6 for more details on such impediments to marriage.) The capacity for marriage is required on the part of both the bride and the groom. If one or both parties lack the capacity to marry, a valid marriage cannot come into existence between the two.

Since marriage may only be entered into willingly, a capable man and a capable woman must each *consent* to the marriage for it to be valid. Consent necessarily implies that they possess a sufficient understanding of what it is they are consenting to. If a party's understanding of marriage is radically different from the Church's understanding, he does not consent to a valid marriage in the eyes of the Church. (Revisit answers 2 and 3 for more details on the essential properties and essential elements of marriage that each spouse must consent to in order for their marriage to be valid.)

These first two requirements for marriage - capacity and consent - are not entirely unique to the Catholic Church, although some of their specific parameters might be (for example, the ages at which a man and a woman may marry). The third way in which a wedding may fail to bring about a valid marriage much more specifically concerns Catholics and non-Catholics wishing to marry Catholics. Other churches and communities may impose their own requirements concerning the manner in which marital consent is to be exchanged, but it is the Catholic canonical form which governs marriages involving even just one Catholic. Unfortunately, this is a requirement that is misunderstood by many today. (Revisit answer 5 for more details.)

Sometimes people will ask, "Where are annulments taught in the Bible?" One possible response is the divorce exception clause discussed in answer 9 (*Mt* 19:9). If "unchastity" in this verse refers to illicit relations between the spouses themselves, then putting an end to those relations via divorce is a good thing. But such a divorce does not end a marriage, because a valid marriage could not have existed in the first place under such circumstances.

14. What are specific *grounds* for annulment?

As we have seen, a marriage may be null for one (or more) of three reasons: lack of capacity, lack of consent, and lack of form. *Capacity* involves a party's ability to contract marriage. *Consent* involves a party's commitment to the marriage as the Church understands it. *Form* has to do with the actual process of entering into marriage (the wedding).

Now we will take a practical look at each of these areas and point out some of the more common grounds on which a marriage tribunal may declare a marriage to be null. Of course, this is not an exhaustive treatment of the subject, but it might be helpful for understanding the concept of an annulment in the Catholic Church.

Lack of capacity generally involves the existence of some diriment impediment. The *Code of Canon Law* identifies many possible impediments to a party's or a couple's capacity to marry. These were discussed in detail in answer 6. Any such factor may constitute grounds for nullity due to lack of capacity.

Lack of consent involves the exclusion, on the part of one or both parties, of some essential property or some essential element of marriage as the Church understands it. If a party does not have at least a similar basic understanding of marriage, he does not enter into marriage validly. But even when a party does possess a sufficient understanding of marriage, if he intentionally excludes an essential property or an essential element of it, he does not sufficiently consent to it. This is grounds for annulment.

The essential *properties* of marriage are unity and indissolubility. Unity means that the marriage is an exclusive relationship between one husband and one wife. Indissolubility means that it is a lifelong commitment between the two. To enter into marriage without the intention of fidelity is to exclude unity, and this exclusion of an essential property of marriage is grounds for annulment. Similarly, a party who weds with the understanding that, if things "don't work out", he can always get a divorce (understood as dissolving the marriage) does not sufficiently consent to marriage. Exclusion of either essential property of marriage is grounds for annulment. (For more details on the essential properties of marriage, see answer 2.)

The essential *elements* of marriage include (among other things) its being ordered to the procreation and education of children. A party who weds with the intent always to exclude from the relationship its ordering to procreation invalidly marries. This doesn't mean the spouses can never choose to regulate procreation (through moral means; see *CCC* 2368) in order to space the births of their children, but it does mean that a valid marriage is incompatible with the wilful exclusion of procreation altogether. In the case of sterility (not impotence), a marriage may still be ordered to procreation if the spouses do not wilfully exclude the right to potentially procreative acts even though it is known in advance that the couple is infertile. Additionally, the education of one's future children - including their religious education - must not be excluded. Therefore, the intention to positively exclude the religious education of offspring is grounds for annulment. (For more details on the essential elements of marriage see answer 3.)

There are many other factors which may be recognised as impeding a person's consent to marriage. For example, since each party must *freely* consent to marriage, anyone *forced* into a marriage does not enter into it with sufficient consent. Thus, a true "shotgun wedding" does not result in a valid marriage. *Fear* that impedes a party's judgement may also be sufficient to invalidate a marriage. Such fear may come into play, for example, in the case of an out-of-wedlock pregnancy, especially involving a very young couple. Force and fear, then, may be grounds for annulment.

Lack of form involves the wedding itself. When a Catholic party gets married, he ordinarily must have a Catholic wedding ceremony in order for his marriage to be valid. The *Code of Canon Law* states, "The form...must be observed if at least one of the parties contracting the marriage was baptised in the Catholic Church or received into it" (1117). Thus, failure of a Catholic to observe canonical form can be grounds for annulment. (For more on lack of form see answer 5.) Additionally, if a Catholic wishes to marry a non-Christian, he must first obtain a dispensation from his bishop in order for his marriage to be valid. Failure of the Catholic party to obtain a dispensation before entering into such a marriage impedes a valid marriage from coming into existence. As such, it constitutes grounds for annulment.

Finally, it should be noted here that a party seeking an annulment is not obliged to determine precisely on which grounds a valid marriage was impeded from coming into existence. He can and should co-operate with the marriage tribunal's inquiry and remember that the ultimate determination of grounds for annulment rests with the Church. Although there may be multiple grounds that could be considered, determination of a single invalidating factor is all that is necessary for a declaration of nullity.

Grounds for nullity may be applicable to only one party, but that is all it takes to declare a marriage null.

Indeed, a marriage tribunal may identify a single factor that can be quickly and easily ruled on and, therefore, not consider any other factors. For example, in the case of a lack of form, the documentary process is often abbreviated.

15. What *aren't* grounds for annulment?

When a person petitions for an annulment, an investigation into the validity of the marriage begins. With enough pertinent information, the experts - i.e., the marriage tribunal - will be able to determine whether the marriage is valid. If the marriage is *not* valid, a declaration of nullity is issued. Conversely, if the marriage *is* valid, a declaration of nullity is not issued. Keep in mind that the purpose of the annulment process is to determine the validity or nullity of a marriage, not to *nullify* a marriage. The Church is powerless to nullify a valid, consummated Christian marriage. A person may believe that he has grounds for annulment (see answer 14), but it is up to the marriage tribunal to determine whether he really does.

It is important to note that grounds for annulment are present, if at all, at the time consent is exchanged. Similar factors that show up later in the marriage do not, of themselves, constitute grounds for annulment. For example, consider adultery. One of the most common causes of divorce is marital infidelity. When a person is married to a spouse who will not remain faithful, it can be a reasonable decision for the innocent spouse to choose civil divorce as a way to protect himself, his children, or his assets (see answer 8). Although some marriages recover from such situations, most do not, and an innocent spouse might wish the marriage itself could be dissolved. But if it is a valid, consummated Christian marriage, no human power can dissolve or nullify it.

A case of adultery is no exception (see answer 9). Of itself, it does not constitute grounds for annulment. It could be that the cheating spouse entered the marriage intending to uphold marriage's essential property of unity (see answer 2) but failed to remain faithful in that regard. Indeed, a spouse who intends on the wedding day to remain always faithful might change his mind later on. So a spouse's infidelity years into the marriage does not necessarily mean that the marriage is null. On the other hand, the marriage tribunal might consider unfaithfulness at any point in the marriage to be *evidence* of a spouse's exclusion of the property of unity at the time the marriage was contracted, and the marriage may thereby be declared null. Such matters belong to the sole determination of the tribunal.

In fact, until a marriage tribunal has determined the nullity of a marriage, everyone should presume it is valid. The *Code of Canon Law* states, "Marriage possesses the favour of law; therefore, in a case of doubt, the validity of a marriage must be upheld until the contrary is proven"

(1060). This means that a divorced person is no more free to date other people than a happily married spouse. His marriage - however difficult the relationship has become - must continue to be considered valid until the marriage tribunal has determined otherwise.

There are some factors that might seem on the surface to be grounds for annulment but are actually not always such. Consider, for example, the *identity* of the person one consents to marry. On the one hand, a person cannot accidentally marry the wrong person. Indeed, the *Code of Canon Law* explicitly states this: "Error concerning the person renders a marriage invalid" (1097 §1). But on the other hand, what about the case of someone who marries the correct person only to find out later that his *character* is different from what it was believed to be at the time of the wedding? Such an error does not always impede a valid marriage from coming into existence. The *Code* states, "Error concerning a quality of the person does not render a marriage invalid even if it is the cause for the contract, unless this quality is directly and principally intended" (1097 §2). In other words, unless some specific quality in a spouse is so important to a person that his consent to marriage depends on it, its absence at the time of the wedding does not invalidate the marriage. For example, unless a person's consent to marriage is so dependent upon his spouse's being a Christian that he would not consent to the marriage otherwise, the fact that his spouse is not a

Christian does not impede a valid marriage. In such a case, the fact that the spouse is not a Christian is not, of itself, grounds for annulment.

This might all seem quite complex - a matter best left to the experts. Indeed, it should be. The best approach in the case of a failed marriage is to petition for annulment (see answer 16) and then rely on the marriage tribunal's expertise to determine whether the marriage is valid or null. And again, until the marriage is declared null, one should always presume that it is valid.

16. What is it like to go through the annulment process?

You may have heard horror stories about the annulment process, how difficult it is to apply, how much it costs, how long it takes, etc. Undoubtedly, the procedure has been in need of reform for quite some time, and Pope Francis recently met this need. The new reforms aim to make the process more streamlined and readily accessible.

Pope Francis issued two documents, *Mitis Iudex Dominus Iesus* ("The Lord Jesus, the Gentle Judge") for the Western church and *Mitis et Misericors Iesus* ("Gentle and Merciful Jesus") for the Eastern Catholic churches, each reforming the applicable code of canon law. Also included are procedural rules that explain how the reforms are to make the annulment process more accessible, less time-consuming, and minimal in costs. The goal is not to grant more annulments, but to speed up and simplify the annulment process without threatening the integrity of marriage. Pope Francis writes, "We have done this following in the footsteps of our predecessors who wished cases of nullity to be handled in a judicial rather than an administrative way, not because the nature of the matter demands it, but rather due to the unparalleled need to safeguard the truth of the sacred bond: something ensured by the judicial order" (*Mitis Iudex*).

A marriage tribunal typically will not accept a petition for nullity until a civil divorce has been finalised. Indeed, the *Code of Canon Law* states, "The judge, before he accepts a case, must be informed that the marriage has irreparably failed, such that conjugal living cannot be restored" (1675). Once a husband and wife have divorced, one or both of them may choose to contact an appropriate diocese, ordinarily with the assistance of a local parish church, to begin the annulment process. The *Code* points out three diocesan tribunals (besides the Apostolic See) competent to hear annulment cases: "the tribunal of the place in which the marriage was celebrated; the tribunal of the place in which either or both parties have a domicile or a quasi-domicile; the tribunal of the place in which in fact most of the proofs must be collected" (1672). Thus, when deciding where to open an annulment case, there may be a variety of options to consider.

Each annulment case is unique, so there is no set time frame within which to expect the process to conclude. That said, the recent reforms have expanded the procedural options from two to three (see next paragraph) and assured that each process is more efficient than before. Additionally, only a single judgement is now necessary for a declaration of nullity to be issued, whereas previously there was an automatic appeal of the tribunal's decision and an annulment was granted only if the second tribunal agreed with the first.

Prior to the reform, only two procedural options for annulment cases were available: first, the ordinary process, in which the applicant had to complete questionnaires, provide certain witnesses, and give testimony and other evidence for the tribunal to consider; second, a shorter "documentary" process involving just the submission of specific documents to prove nullity (for example, documents proving that a Catholic did not observe the canonical form of marriage). The reformed process now includes a third, streamlined process in which any simple case may be presented directly to the bishop for his decision. Canon 1683 notes that this process may be used whenever "the petition is proposed by both spouses or by one of them, with the consent of the other," and "circumstance of things and persons recur, with substantiating testimonies and records, which do not demand a more accurate inquiry or investigation, and which render the nullity manifest." Additionally, the new procedural rules outlined by Pope

Francis provide examples of circumstances under which this new streamlined process may be used:

> The defect of faith which can generate simulation of consent or error that determines the will; a brief conjugal cohabitation; an abortion procured to avoid procreation; an obstinate persistence in an extra-conjugal relationship at the time of the wedding or immediately following it; the deceitful concealment of sterility, or grave contagious illness, or children from a previous relationship, or incarcerations; a cause of marriage completely extraneous to married life, or consisting of the unexpected pregnancy of the woman, physical violence inflicted to extort consent, the defect of the use of reason which is proved by medical documents, etc. (*Mitis Iudex*).

Upon the declaration of nullity, the parties are ordinarily free to marry other people. Canon 1682 states, "After the sentence declaring the nullity of the marriage has become effective, the parties whose marriage has been declared null can contract a new marriage unless a prohibition attached to the sentence itself or established by the local ordinary forbids this."

Having said all this, it is important to emphasise that the reforms to the annulment process are not intended to open the door to a "rubber stamp" mentality for the declaration of nullity. Pope Francis's procedural rules stress this point: "To achieve the moral certainty required by law, a preponderance of proofs and indications is not sufficient, but it is required that any prudent doubt of making an error, in law or in fact, is excluded, even if the mere possibility of the contrary is not removed" (*Mitis Iudex*).

17. What about attending weddings?

Catholics are sometimes faced with the difficult decision of whether to attend the wedding of a friend or relative whose marriage clearly will not be valid. For example, it might be the wedding of a lapsed Catholic getting married outside the Church without a dispensation from canonical form (see answer 5), or of a divorced Catholic getting remarried without an annulment (see answer 10). In either case, the wedding clearly will not result in a valid marriage, yet the couple will begin living together and expecting others to treat them as though they *are* validly married. What is a faithful Catholic to do?

The Catholic Church does not explicitly address the question of whether or not to attend a wedding that will not result in a valid marriage, but it does more broadly address the matter of words and attitudes that encourage and confirm others in objectively wrong behaviour. The *Catechism* states,

Every word or attitude is forbidden which by flattery, adulation, or complaisance encourages and confirms another in malicious acts and perverse conduct. Adulation is a grave fault if it makes one an accomplice in another's vices or grave sins. Neither the desire to be of service nor friendship justifies duplicitous speech. Adulation is a venial sin when it only seeks to be agreeable, to avoid evil, to meet a need, or to obtain legitimate advantages (2480).

Additionally, the danger of scandal (leading others into sin) must be considered. What would attendance at the wedding say to the couple and to others? The *Catechism* explains,

> Scandal is an attitude or behaviour which leads another to do evil. The person who gives scandal becomes his neighbour's tempter. He damages virtue and integrity; he may even draw his brother into spiritual death. Scandal is a grave offense if by deed or omission another is deliberately led into a grave offense. Scandal takes on a particular gravity by reason of the authority of those who cause it or the weakness of those who are scandalised. It prompted our Lord to utter this curse: "Whoever causes one of these little ones who believe in me to sin, it would be better for him to have a great millstone fastened round his neck and to be drowned in the depth of the sea" (*Mt* 18:6; see also *1 Co* 8:10-13). Scandal is grave when given by those who by nature or office are obliged to teach and educate others. Jesus reproaches the scribes and Pharisees on this account: he likens them to wolves in sheep's clothing (2284-2285).

In consideration of all this, I cannot recommend attending any wedding that will not result in a valid marriage. Instead, I suggest charitably explaining the reasons for declining the invitation, as well as expressing hope and offering guidance for the couple in amending their plans.

Will this approach, one might naturally ask, put a strain on relationships or even cause one to lose contact with friends or relatives who resent one's choice not to attend a wedding? It is important to remember that the difficulty of the situation has been brought about by the fallen-away Catholic, not the person foregoing the wedding festivities on moral grounds. Keep in mind that when a lapsed Catholic attempts to sever his relationship with the Church, he should recognise that there will be consequences for his decision. Family members and friends who remain faithful to Christ and his Church will not take the decision lightly.

People sometimes argue that it is acceptable to attend a wedding just for the purpose of maintaining a relationship in the interest of bringing a fallen-away Catholic back to the Church. They assert that attending a wedding that will not result in a valid marriage is acceptable whenever *not* attending it would hinder one's influence over the fallen-away Catholic, thus lessening the chances of his future reversion to the Faith. This reasoning sounds perilously close to choosing to do evil (supporting another in sin) so that good may result from it (influence is maintained). The *Catechism* addresses such an attitude:

> It is therefore an error to judge the morality of human acts by considering only the intention that inspires them or the circumstances (environment, social pressure, duress or emergency, etc.) which supply their context. There are acts which, in and of themselves, independently of circumstances and intentions, are always gravely illicit by reason of their object; such as blasphemy and perjury, murder and adultery. One may not do evil so that good may result from it (1756).

On a final note, direction from an orthodox Catholic spiritual director is often a good idea in such difficult situations. Spiritual direction can help ensure that one's obligations to family and friends are wisely met without contravening God's laws.

18. What about *same-sex* weddings?

It should be clear from answers 1 and 3 that same-sex relationships are simply never capable of being marriages at all. God created man "male and female" (*Gn* 1:27; 2:24) so that husband and wife may bond with each other and engage in procreative activity. To begin with, two people of the same sex do not complement one another in the way that is necessary for procreative activity. Based on this fact alone, same-sex relationships are not - indeed, cannot ever be - marriages. But there is more to this question for Christians.

Marriage must emulate the relationship between Christ and his Church (see answer 1). In part, this means that in addition to its ordination to procreation, it must be ordered to the *good* of the spouses; both purposes are *essential* elements of marriage (see answer 3). And just as Christ makes the Church holy, spouses are to help each other be holy for ultimate union with Christ in heaven (see *CCC* 1644). They must will one another's true good and make each other's salvation a primary end of the relationship itself. To this end, they must view moral issues as the Church views them.

The Church's teaching on the morality of sexual relationships between persons of the same sex is clear and consistent: they are always *immoral*. The *Catechism* teaches,

> Basing itself on Sacred Scripture, which presents homosexual acts as acts of grave depravity, tradition has always declared that homosexual acts are intrinsically disordered. They are contrary to the natural law. They close the sexual act to the gift of life. They do not proceed from a genuine affective and sexual complementarity. Under no circumstances can they be approved (2357).

Notice that this teaching is based on Sacred Scripture. In the New Testament, it is primarily in St Paul's letters that same-sex relationships are directly condemned. Paul calls them "unnatural" and points out that there are "penalties" associated with them (*Rm* 1:26-27). Indeed, when writing to the Corinthians, Paul clarifies that one penalty for homosexual acts is the loss of salvation (*1 Co* 6:9-10). Therefore, partners in a same-sex relationship are doing just the opposite of "good" for one another. In reality, they are putting the gratification of their own unnatural desires first, without regard to each other's relationship with Christ. Thus, they are not truly helping each other to be holy for ultimate union with Christ in heaven. They do not authentically will one another's *true* good by making each other's salvation a primary end of the relationship. Having said all this, it is important to make a distinction between same-sex attractions and homosexual acts. Any attraction, of itself, is not sinful. It is merely an *inclination* toward sin. But because this particular inclination cannot ever be fulfilled morally, a person must resist it. Difficult as this may be, it is not an impossible or even unrealistic proposition. Jesus said, "If any man would come after me, let him deny himself and take up his cross and follow me" (*Mt* 16:24). The *Catechism*, acknowledging that same-sex attraction is "a trial", instructs, "Homosexual persons are called to chastity. By the virtues of self-mastery that teach them inner freedom, at times by the support of disinterested friendship, by prayer and sacramental grace, they can and should gradually and resolutely approach Christian perfection" (2359).

The *Catechism* also exhorts Christians to treat people with same-sex attraction appropriately, just as they should treat *anyone* afflicted with a disordered desire, especially when salvation is at risk: "They must be accepted with respect, compassion, and sensitivity. Every sign of unjust discrimination in their regard should be avoided. These persons are called to fulfil God's will in their lives and, if they are Christians, to unite to the sacrifice of the Lord's cross the difficulties they may encounter from their condition" (2358).

Thus, same-sex unions are never truly marriages at all, no matter what people might call them. Quite to the contrary, they are offenses against chastity as well as the dignity of the institution of marriage itself. It should be evident, then, that consideration of weddings, marriages, divorces, and annulments are really quite irrelevant when it comes to same-sex relationships. Indeed, it could be argued that something similar to the "exception clause" discussed in answer 9 could be applied to same-sex "marriages", seeing as same-sex relations are always unchaste and should therefore cease.

19. What are other offenses against the dignity of marriage?

Once a person understands what true marriage is and how it must mirror Christ's relationship with his Church, it becomes easy to recognise activities and relationships that offend against it. We have already seen that adultery (answer 2), divorce (answer 8), and same-sex unions (answer 18) are offenses against the dignity of marriage. In actuality, *any* sexual relationship that exists apart from the conjugal union of a validly married husband and wife is an offence against the dignity of marriage. The *Catechism* teaches,

> The sexual act must take place exclusively within marriage. Outside of marriage it always constitutes a grave sin and excludes one from sacramental communion... Carnal union is morally legitimate only when a definitive community of life between a man and woman has been established...
>
> It demands a total and definitive gift of persons to one another (2390-91).

The *Catechism* points out several common offenses against the dignity of marriage: polygamy, incest, sexual abuse, free union (e.g., living together), as well as additional related offenses (2387-91).

For example, since an essential property of marriage is the *unity* of one man and one woman, polygamy is clearly an offense against marriage. The *Catechism* states, "Conjugal communion is radically contradicted by polygamy; this, in fact, directly negates the plan of God which was revealed from the beginning, because it is contrary to the equal personal dignity of men and women who in matrimony give themselves with a love that is total and therefore unique and exclusive" (2387).

It was noted in answer 6 that marriages between family members too closely related to each other (usually first cousins or closer) are invalid. This being the case, any sort of sexual relationship between such relatives constitutes an offense against the institution of marriage. The *Catechism* explains,

Incest designates intimate relations between relatives or in-laws within a degree that prohibits marriage between them. St Paul stigmatises this especially grave offense: "It is actually reported that there is immorality among you...for a man is living with his father's wife... In the name of the Lord Jesus...you are to deliver this man to Satan for the destruction of the flesh" (*1 Co* 5:1, 4-5). Incest corrupts family relationships and marks a regression towards animality (2388).

Similarly, the abuse of children is a reprehensible offense against marriage. The *Catechism* teaches,

Connected to incest is any sexual abuse perpetrated by adults on children or adolescents entrusted to their care. The offense is compounded by the scandalous harm done to the physical and moral integrity of the young, who will remain scarred by it all their lives; and the violation of responsibility for their upbringing (2389).

Some couples choose to live together freely as though they are married but without the lifelong commitment and the property of indissolubility essential to marriage. This, of course, is an offense against marriage. The *Catechism* notes,

> In a so-called *free union*, a man and a woman refuse to give juridical and public form to a liaison involving sexual intimacy. The expression "free union" is fallacious: what can "union" mean when the partners make no commitment to one another, each exhibiting a lack of trust in the other, in himself, or in the future?
>
> The expression covers a number of different situations: concubinage, rejection of marriage as such, or inability to make long-term commitments. All these situations offend against the dignity of marriage; they destroy the very idea of the family; they weaken the sense of fidelity. They are contrary to the moral law (2390).

Just short of "free union" is the situation of a couple living together before they get married. It is a sort of test drive before the actual purchase. Of course, such a relationship cannot provide the assurances and securities that marriage provides, and so it often ends long before the wedding date (if such a date was even established). The *Catechism* explains,

> Some today claim a *"right to a trial marriage"* where there is an intention of getting married later. However firm the purpose of those who engage in premature sexual relations may be, the fact is that such liaisons can scarcely ensure mutual sincerity and fidelity in a relationship between a man and a woman, nor, especially, can they protect it from inconstancy of desires or whim... Human love does not tolerate "trial marriages" (2391).

20. What can a husband and wife do to ensure that their marriage is valid and divorce-proof?

Every Catholic who would like to plan a wedding should contact his local parish church well in advance of setting a date to allow time for certain preparations to be made. The Church needs to ascertain that there are no impediments to the marriage and that each party is adequately prepared to freely enter into this new covenantal relationship with a sufficient understanding of what marriage is. Following the guidance of the local church will ensure that canonical form is observed and that any necessary dispensations are taken care of at the appropriate times. These are the first steps to ensuring that a valid marriage comes into existence on the wedding day.

But the wedding day is just the beginning! Just as Christian marriage emulates the relationship between Christ and his Church (see answer 1), so the *family* (i.e., the spouses along with their children) goes on to form a microcosm of the Church. This view of the family explains why it has been referred to since ancient times as the "domestic church"; it is part of God's plan for humanity. Indeed, as the *Catechism* notes, "Christ chose to be born and grow up in the bosom of the holy family of Joseph and Mary" (1655). In a similar way, the Church itself, built on individual Christian families, grows as Christ's own family. The *Catechism* continues,

> The Church is nothing other than the family of God. From the beginning, the core of the Church was often constituted by those who had become believers "together with all [their] household" (see *Ac* 18:8). When they were converted, they desired that "their whole household" should also be saved (see *Ac* 11:14; *Ac* 16:31). These families who became believers were islands of Christian life in an unbelieving world (1655).

Still today, Christian families are individual cells of the Mystical Body itself. Indeed, the Church is built on these families that individually reflect the whole. Every Christian family is, in a real sense, a miniature church in which an indissoluble covenant exists for the good of the spouses and their children as they journey to heaven (see answers 2 and 3). The *Catechism* teaches, "The Christian family constitutes a specific revelation and realisation of ecclesial communion... It is a community of faith, hope, and charity" (2204).

Given that the good of the spouses - an essential element of marriage (see answer 3) - is primarily a matter of their salvation, it naturally follows that the spouses' love for their children must be similarly focused on their children's salvation, (through their union with Christ).

As such, the Church may be seen as the ultimate image of the family, the exemplar that the family must imitate. The *Catechism* teaches, "The Christian family...is called to partake of the prayer and sacrifice of Christ. Daily prayer and the reading of the word of God strengthen it in charity. The Christian family has an evangelising and missionary task" (2205).

Knowing this task in advance, spouses should prepare their home, as a church in miniature, to be the place where their children first experience and grow in the life of the larger Church. This life begins with family prayer. The *Catechism* teaches,

> The *Christian family* is the first place of education in prayer. Based on the sacrament of marriage, the family is the "domestic church" where God's children learn to pray as the Church and to persevere in prayer. For young children in particular, daily family prayer is the

first witness of the Church's living memory as awakened patiently by the Holy Spirit (2685).

Grounded in prayer, the family grows primarily as part of the kingdom of God, not of this world. It is a safe haven where each person develops in relationship with Christ. The *Catechism* explains:

In our own time, in a world often alien and even hostile to faith, believing families are of primary importance as centres of living, radiant faith. For this reason the Second Vatican Council, using an ancient expression, calls the family the *Ecclesia domestic* (see *Lumen Gentium* 11; see *Familiaris Consortio* 21). It is in the bosom of the family that parents are "by word and example...the first heralds of the Faith with regard to their children. They should encourage them in the vocation which is proper to each child, fostering with special care any religious vocation" (*Lumen Gentium* 11) (1656).

Finally, it is within the family that children become active in living authentic Christian lives. The *Catechism* states, "Here one learns endurance and the joy of work, fraternal love, generous - even repeated - forgiveness, and above all divine worship in prayer and the offering of one's life" (1657).

Approaching marriage and the family in this way - as the domestic church - helps to ensure that the spouses do not lose sight of the beautiful reality that their marriage truly is. Selfishness recedes as their love for each other and their children matures. St Paul describes such love this way:

Love is patient and kind; love is not jealous or boastful; it is not arrogant or rude. Love does not insist on its own way; it is not irritable or resentful; it does not rejoice at wrong, but rejoices in the right. Love bears all things, believes all things, hopes all things, endures all things. Love never ends (*1 Co* 13:4-8).

These words, put into action, help spouses to love each other and their children authentically and sacramentally. Such love, indeed, makes marriage divorce-proof.